Notting Hill

Notting Hill

Derry Moore

F

FRANCES LINCOLN LIMITED
PUBLISHERS

For Marina,
whose idea this book was

Frances Lincoln Limited
4 Torriano Mews
Torriano Avenue
London NW5 2RZ
www.franceslincoln.com

Notting Hill
Copyright © Frances Lincoln Limited
2007
Text and photographs
copyright © Derry Moore 2007

Derry Moore has asserted his moral right
to be identified as the author of this work
in accordance with the Copyright,
Designs and Patents Act 1988 (UK).

British Library Cataloguing in
Publication Data
A catalogue record for this book is
available from the British Library.

ISBN 978-0-7112-2739-2

Designed by Becky Clarke
Printed and bound in Singapore

9 8 7 6 5 4 3 2 1

Contents

Introduction

I have lived in Notting Hill for more than twenty-five years. When, in 1979, my wife and I bought a house here, few people had heard of Ledbury Road and persuading a bank to grant a mortgage proved unusually difficult, since we were to be above a shop. At that time most of the ground floors of the houses at the southern end of Ledbury Road were occupied by antique shops; now, as is the way when districts become fashionable, the ubiquitous boutiques have moved in, driving out the antique shops, rather like grey squirrels driving out the indigenous red ones. Perhaps not a strictly accurate analogy, since so many of the antique shops were owned by Italians and, of the remaining three, two belong to Italians still. All three have been able to stay because they own the freehold of their shops – and the dwellings above – having bought these well before the surge in prices over the past twenty years.

It was while taking the photographs for this book that I tried to analyse the secret of the appeal of this district, the place where I was born, as my parents owned a house in Lansdowne Crescent, which they sold in 1947 when I was ten. I also tried to analyse why Notting Hill hasn't always been as popular as it is today and what precisely the area known as Notting Hill consists of.

In London, the boundaries of a borough are clearly defined, whereas those of an area are far more fluid, varying according to time and personal preference; and Notting Hill illustrates this to an unusual extent. As recently as twenty years ago it wouldn't have occurred to someone living in Holland Park, Campden Hill or Ladbroke Grove to say that they lived in Notting Hill, and even those living in what is now considered the heart of Notting Hill would frequently refer to their houses as belonging to one of the adjacent neighbourhoods. The reverse is the case today, as a glance at property advertisements confirms; Notting Hill is now generally accepted as being one of the most desirable parts of London and is most definitely 'in'. Why, one now wonders, was it ever 'out'?

Physically, the Ladbroke estate has not changed significantly since the second half of the nineteenth century. The same squares were there then, the same broad streets, with houses, rarely very tall, generously set back from the pavement – the latter frequently wide, too – all combining to give a feeling of space. The communal gardens were there, with the profusion of trees and greenery that lends almost a country air to the adjacent streets. So also were the houses with stuccoed or partially stuccoed exteriors that so effectively reflect the light. Notting Hill is distinguished by its hilly terrain; and, too, by the absence of a grid plan in the layout of the streets such as that, for example, in Bloomsbury. That late eighteenth-century development by the British Museum – much favoured in the first quarter of the twentieth century by the intellectual group to which it lent its name – provides an interesting comparison with Notting Hill; and it can serve to illuminate some of Notting Hill's particular appeal. Bloomsbury is laid out, on land of unvarying flatness, in classic late-eighteenth-century manner, with uniform terraces of houses with fronts that drop straight down into narrow service areas squeezed in between house and pavement. The houses are mainly built of bare brick, which absorbs rather than reflects the light, and, although there are garden squares, roads run between the squares and the houses, the roads, insatiable as cormorants, waiting to steal ever more of the green space. All this contributes to the extremely urban feeling of Bloomsbury, a place where the countryside seems remote. This cannot have been of great importance in the late eighteenth century, when London was much smaller and the real countryside was more accessible; but it matters today.

Architecturally, Notting Hill cannot pretend to have houses of really great distinction. Even so, they are seldom less than agreeable and, in the best parts of the Ladbroke estate at least, amid their communal gardens they combine to provide some remarkable effects of architectural theatre. What distinguishes the area is its layout. Some of this is the result of deliberate planning – albeit planning at a second or third remove and never fully realized according to the original intention – while much of it has happened by accident, helped by the hilly terrain.

Although Notting Hill's atmosphere reaches well beyond its physical limits, its heart remains the estate acquired in the mid-eighteenth century – when it was mostly open countryside – by the wealthy Ladbroke family: in particular the part, comprising nearly 200 acres, which stretches from Notting Hill Gate in the south to the railway and Westway in the north, to Portobello Road in the east and in the west as far as Notting Dale, beyond Portland Road. Most of this area was taken up by what was briefly, at the end of the 1830s, the racecourse known as the Hippodrome.

During the most significant period of its development – the thirty odd years after 1819 – the Ladbroke estate belonged to James Weller Ladbroke, who had inherited it from a distant cousin. Its layout was the indirect offspring of that most fruitful period of urban planning the very early nineteenth century, when the architect John Nash designed Regent's Park, Regent's Street and the Mall.

In the early nineteenth century the estate was still largely rural and lay just beyond the western limits of London proper. Although Ladbroke himself seems to have taken little direct interest in its development, he engaged a remarkable man as surveyor/architect to plan the development for him: Thomas Allason. Born in 1790, Allason was evidently a man of vision and, like Nash, in addition to being an architect he was a landscape designer; he had also visited Italy in his twenties and published a book of *Picturesque Views of the Antiquities of Pola in Istria*. Being – untypically for London – hilly, the Ladbroke estate offered Allason an exceptional opportunity.

In the early 1820s he drew up a highly ambitious plan for the layout of the estate. In this he was certainly influenced by Nash's plans for Regent's Park, in which private villas were to have been situated in such a way as to give the owners the illusion of living in the countryside, with the outer reaches surrounded by elegant terraces, the idea being to combine the bucolic pleasures of the country with the amenities of the town. Although Allason's plan for the Ladbroke estate, which included an enormous circus at its centre, was never realized – had it been we might have had a second Regent's Park on the west side of London – something of its spirit undoubtedly permeates the area as we know it today, and gives it a touch of elegance and distinction. Two important features of his plan that have survived are the many large communal gardens – 'paddocks', as they were originally known – which were laid out as pleasure gardens for the residents of the surrounding houses; and the large concentric crescents to the west of Ladbroke Grove – Lansdowne Crescent, the west end of Lansdowne Road and Elgin Crescent.

The reasons Allason's original plan failed to be realized are complex. The prime reason was money, or rather lack of money coupled with the fact that there was no long-term credit to be had. Another, importantly, was the fact that long leases for development on the Ladbroke estate were granted not simply to one speculator but to many, resulting in the absence of any single driving force in the whole development.

In 1837 there occurred the curious interlude of the Notting Hill racecourse, the Hippodrome. Superficially the Ladbroke estate must have seemed an ideal place for a racecourse. From its centre, on the rise where St John's Church now stands, spectators could view the entire course and the countryside beyond. Moreover, at that date there were no racecourses nearer to London than Epsom and Ascot, both about twenty miles to the south-west and west of the city. The Hippodrome had the great advantage of being within easy reach of the city for a day's outing. It occupied some 100 acres and stretched north-west from Notting Hill Gate, the entrance being at what is now the junction of Kensington Park Road and Ladbroke Road where a cabdrivers' shelter stands – one of the thirteen that survive of the many built by Lord Shaftesbury in 1875, and a Grade II listed building.

However, the speculative venture of the Hippodrome had a life of only three years. Apart from the fact that the heavy clay soil of Notting Hill was unsuitable for racing – although ideal for the Potteries further down the hill to the west in the area known as Notting Dale – the course was plagued with difficulties, in particular the matter of a right of way that effectively allowed the public to cross the track at will, which they did: often interrupting a race in progress, much to the fury of the spectators. Added to this annoyance was the fact that the course had been built so close to the neighbouring slums of the Potteries and the Piggeries that police had to patrol the grounds to keep 'unsavoury' slum dwellers off the course. Most important of all, following the rapid expansion of the whole of London at this time, the pressure from property speculators eager to take advantage of the expansion to the west proved irresistible, the financial returns from the racecourse being much less attractive than those to be derived from the building and sale of new houses.

The last race meeting at the Hippodrome was held on 4 June 1841 and it was during the subsequent seven years that the area acquired the aspect that it retains to this day. The Ladbrokes, who still owned the freehold of the land occupied by the Hippodrome, as well as the rest of the estate, had granted building agreements to two speculators, Jacob Connop and John Duncan. As a result of this division, Allason had ceased to be the sole man in charge of designing and planning the estate and the venture became one of investment, with the far shorter-term goal of financial return. In addition, both Connop and Duncan, whose optimistic expectations had not been fully realized (Connop went bankrupt in 1845), were obliged to sell off parcels of their land to other speculators, thereby diluting the original ownership even further. Consequently, by the mid-1840s myriad developers were involved in the development of the original Ladbroke estate, each with his own commercial, rather than aesthetic, agenda. Not surprisingly, the result was something of an architectural hotchpotch.

One interesting by-product of this dilution of ownership and the involvement of many different speculators and architects is that although the architecture of Notting Hill lacks the distinction of either Regent's Park or Bath, there is a singular charm in the diversity of its houses and streets. The area has a quirky quality, a haphazard element, typical of much of London but with the important difference that, unlike some other areas developed at the same period, beneath its casual exterior the Ladbroke estate is supported by a formal, architectural scheme; it could be compared to a garden long left untended that has 'good bones' lying below.

It is interesting to trace the various influences – almost genetic – that define the area. Much of the character may be seen as deriving from Bath, that classic example of eighteenth-century urban design, and, perhaps even more directly, from Cheltenham.

One key figure among the early developers in Notting Hill was Pearson Thompson, who in early life had practised as a solicitor in London but had moved to Cheltenham when he inherited his father's extensive property there in 1820. The Thompsons, father and son, employed the distinguished architect J.B. Papworth in the layout and design of their highly successful Cheltenham estates, and the spirit and character of much of his work in that town may be seen in what was to follow in Notting Hill. While a superficial influence may be noted in some of the street names, in particular the many Lansdownes (Lansdowne Road, Lansdowne Crescent, Lansdowne Rise, Lansdowne Walk, etc.) that found their way to Ladbroke's estate from Bath via Cheltenham, a more important influence was that of James Thomson, who, in addition to being the articled pupil of J.B. Papworth, had worked under Nash on some of the terraces in Regent's Park. Thomson was employed on an important section of the layout around the high ground where St John's Church now stands. From this high point on a clear day in the 1840s could be seen St Paul's Cathedral to the east and even Windsor Castle, twenty miles away to the west. In this area one can trace the influence both of Bath, with its alternation of curving crescents built on hills, straight roads and large gardens, and of Regent's Park, with its aspiration of creating a *rus in urbe*. When Thomson submitted a plan for his intentions it was entitled 'a Plan of Kensington Park, Notting Hill, as designed and laid out for building, with ornamental grounds, public drives etc., etc.'. The fact that ornamental grounds and public drives were included in the plan suggests ambitions beyond those of a purely commercial nature and, possibly, a sense of the need to enhance the district where people were to live beyond merely providing houses. It was James Thomson who first turned Thomas Allason's original idea of shared private gardens into practical form and it was he who developed the idea of the concentric crescents to the north-west of the hill where St John's now stands.

Among the various speculators involved in the development of the Ladbroke estate, one of the few who were successful was Charles Henry Blake. The son of a man who had made money as a captain of ships plying the India run and then as an indigo planter in Bengal in the late eighteenth century, Blake returned to England in the early 1840s, after selling the indigo business that he inherited. He invested in land on the Ladbroke estate and employed as his architect Thomas Allom. Allom was not only an architect but also a well-known landscape artist who, like Allason, had travelled extensively in Italy. He planned the area where Stanley Crescent and Kensington Park Gardens now stand. Looking down Stanley Crescent from Kensington Park Gardens one can detect his artist's vision in the almost theatrical view, with its hints of hidden space and vistas that lie beyond – vistas that, as in a theatre, are suggested, rather than actually existing. Allom also built some of the most distinctive houses in the neighbourhood, notably the largest house, on the corner of Kensington Park Gardens and Ladbroke Grove, built for his employer. The originality of his design can be seen by comparing Allom's houses to some of those that form a terrace on the south side of Ladbroke Square. In these, built in the early 1840s, traces can still be seen of the eighteenth-century Georgian tradition with its restraint and, one might almost say, modesty, whereas the houses around Stanley Crescent are more flamboyant and exploit a generous use of stucco.

Allom also designed St Peter's Church in Kensington Park Road, which looks up Stanley Gardens to the middle of Stanley Crescent. This church is one of the few built in the classical style after the 1830s, when the fashionable style for ecclesiastical building was Gothic, considered more ancient and sacred in mid-nineteenth-century England than the classical style. St Peter's has a theatricality that has earned it the sobriquet of a taste of Borromini in the west of London. Interestingly, the 'Gothic' churches now look less genuine than St Peter's: they look newer, more like pastiches and not at all truly Gothic. There are a number of churches in the area; the proximity of a church seems to have been an important ingredient in the success of a district in mid-nineteenth-century England. Some of these churches are quite grand, such as St Peter's, or St John's in Lansdowne Crescent, which has the most impressive situation of them all.

It is interesting to note the type of residents who first occupied the houses in and around the Ladbroke estate. A contemporary survey of the residents around Pembridge Square (to the east of the Ladbroke estate), who were of a similar social type to those of the Ladbroke estate, includes several returned from India, one being a major general in the service of the East India Company, a West Indies 'proprietor', a stockbroker, a colliery owner, a publisher, a bookseller, a chintz printer and several lawyers. It should also be noted that at least a third of the occupants of the houses were servants, who lived in the attics. The latter were not allowed in the private squares unless accompanying their employers or their employers' children. One of the best-known figures around Pembridge Square was Field Marshal Sir John Burgoyne, who had served in the Peninsular Wars under Wellington, in the American war of 1812 and in the Crimea. At the end of his life he lived in the square, and he died there in 1871 at the then great age of eighty-nine. There were no what might be termed hereditary 'grandees', the latter generally having country estates and wanting their London places of residence to be more 'in town' and nearer to Parliament.

The Notting Hill area had one big financial advantage, which was simply that one could get more land for one's money: in Pimlico, for example, in the 1820s and 1830s Thomas Cubitt was paying £50 per acre, while as late as 1846 the Ladbrokes were selling land for only £30 per acre. This figure also helps to explain the generous use of land, making possible the creation of no less than fifteen communal gardens.

As well as the various sizeable churches of Notting Hill there remain today many non-sectarian places of worship, which are a testimony to the history of the darker side of Notting Hill, in districts such as the Potteries in Notting Dale. Located just a few hundred yards to the west of the prosperous Ladbroke estate, so near as to be almost a part of Notting Hill, the Potteries was regarded during much of the nineteenth century as one of the worst slums – if not the very worst – in London. In an article written in the late 1840s in a publication called *Household Words* Charles Dickens wrote: 'In a neighbourhood studded thickly with elegant villas and mansions, viz.: Bayswater and Notting Hill, in the parish of Kensington, is a plague-spot, scarcely equalled for its insalubrity by any other in London; it is called the Potteries.' There was evidently insufficient sewerage or drainage, and filth, disease and lack of sanitation gave the area a 'notoriety unsurpassed in any other part of London'. It is difficult to imagine the parallel lives that were lived so close together.

The Potteries, as its name denotes, was devoted to the manufacture of goods made from clay. The kilns were established in the first quarter of the nineteenth century. It must not be imagined that the goods produced here were exquisite figurines, jugs or bowls – this was no Chelsea or Bow porcelain factory; rather, drainpipes, household bricks, tiles and flower pots were the main output produced in Notting Dale, over an area of 16 acres.

The district was also where the dispossessed pig farmers of Tyburnia had moved after their land in Paddington was taken for development in the 1820s. From then until the 1870s the Potteries were also used for the farming of pigs – a clause in the original leases included the item 'for the purposes of pig-keeping'. This involved not only the raising of pigs but also the preparation of pigswash, a mixture of entrails, offal and refuse, all decomposing; this was collected from hotels and clubhouses and boiled in coppers at the Piggeries. The disgusting smell can be imagined. In the 1860s there were as many pigs as people living there together, the pigs undoubtedly making their modest contribution to the squalor, as well as to the pot. Rough cottages, sheds and shanties were built, many of them over stagnant pools of water, and many dwellings were simply made out of converted derelict railway carriages.

Not surprisingly, when cholera struck in London, in December 1847, the Potteries proved fertile ground. To read about this area is like reading about the bustees of Bombay or Calcutta; even by the end of the nineteenth century the death rate in the Potteries was still scandalously high, 432 children out of every 1,000 dying before the age of one, compared to 161 per 1,000 in London as a whole. The Reverend Charles Booth, founder of the Salvation Army, who made an extensive study of the poorer districts in the metropolis, wrote that the poverty in the Potteries was 'of as dark and deep a type as anywhere in London'. The average life expectancy among the inhabitants of the Potteries in 1846–8 was 11 years and 7 months, as against an average of 37 years in the rest of London, and it was not until 1923 that the borough council decided that landlords should be required to provide a water closet for every twelve people, as well as a proper water supply.

Curiously, the proximity of the Potteries does not seem to have affected those living in the smarter parts of the district and, so far as I have been able to discover, it is never quoted as a cause for the decline in popularity of the prosperous Ladbroke estate. However, decline the estate did, from the end of the First World War, and it remained out of favour with the properous classes until the second half of the 1960s.

The reasons for this falling off are not entirely clear, but they were probably part of a larger pattern. The Great War, in which approximately one million people from Great Britain were killed, was followed by the calamitous flu epidemic of 1918, which killed another two hundred thousand. In 1921 there was a serious crash on the London Stock Exchange, which ruined many people. Many of those who owned the large houses in Kensington Park Gardens and the vicinity could no longer afford to keep what they regarded as the necessary number of servants; nor could they afford properly to maintain the houses, which started to suffer from dry rot, cracking stucco and the general wear and tear from which all houses need to be protected. The Wall Street crash of 1929 caused yet more devastation. During the depression that followed in its wake, many of the houses in Notting Hill were sold to developers and builders. They were then converted into flats and bed-sits, almost invariably in the worst possible (and cheapest) taste, with the result that the value of the properties depreciated even further. Side by side with the deterioration of the buildings went the decay of the gardens, which were no longer properly cared for.

This state of affairs continued throughout the thirties and during and after the Second World War, when obtaining building materials was a problem. In addition, the enormous rise in the rate of taxation imposed by the new Labour government in the years after 1945 severely affected the professional and middle classes, from whose ranks had come the principal residents of the Ladbroke estate.

By the late 1940s the very name of Notting Hill evoked a down-at-heel area of cheap lodgings, and the general decline was exacerbated by the influx of immigrants from the Caribbean after the Second World War, with the first immigrants arriving on SS *Windrush* in 1948. This new group of residents in need of housing was immediately exploited by unscrupulous landlords. One of them, Peter Rachman, who was particularly active in the area around Paddington and Notting Hill, was so notorious that Rachmanism became an accepted term to describe the activity of unprincipled landlords.

Interestingly, Rachman was himself an immigrant, having been born in Poland in 1920, the son of a Jewish dentist; he escaped the Nazis, but spent a horrific time in a Russian labour camp before fleeing to England in 1946. After various menial jobs he entered the property world in the 1950s, borrowing money to buy his first building, a lodging house north of the Harrow Road. He was able to get this very cheaply because seven out of the eight rooms were let to 'sitting tenants', who could not be evicted and whose low rents were protected by law. Knowing that the rents would become decontrolled as soon as the tenants vacated their homes, Rachman let the eighth room to a group of Caribbean musicians and encouraged them to make as much noise as possible, night and day. Unsurprisingly, after three months Rachman was in possession of an empty building and free to charge new tenants whatever rents he wished.

This method became the blueprint for a formula he pursued with great financial success, buying occupied buildings and then inducing the tenants to leave by the use of very dubious tactics, including not only playing loud music, but also leaving building repairs undone – on one occasion he went so far as to have the roof removed – utilities cut off and any other form of general harassment that he could come up with. The new tenants of Rachman's properties were, for the most part, newly arrived immigrants, who were easy to exploit, as the prejudice of the time made it particularly difficult for them to find rental accommodation. Desperate West Indian families were willing to pay extortionate rents for the privilege of being crammed into tiny apartments.

Thus began a vicious cycle. There was bitter resentment on the part of poor white people, who now had difficulty finding both accommodation and jobs, which they felt had been taken from them by the black immigrants. This resentment was exploited by groups such as Keep Britain White, which, in a campaign organized by Oswald Mosley, instigated demonstrations and marches in Notting Hill of white youths who, wielding bicycle chains and other weapons, threatened the residents and attacked those who resisted. Blacks groups retaliated. The police were obliged to intervene; however, there was a perception on the part of the black population that the police were prejudiced against them. This cycle eventually led to the Notting Hill race riots of 1958.

It was partly as a consequence of this situation and the desire to defuse it that the Notting Hill Carnival was started in 1965. This now famous annual event was – and is – a Caribbean occasion. Although started as a local affair by the West Indian residents of the area, it now attracts around a million people when it takes place over the August Bank Holiday weekend. The streets in Notting Hill become like Trinidad at carnival time, with stalls selling jerk pork and chicken, salt fish, black-eyed peas and rice, and other Caribbean delicacies. The preparation of the costumes and floats is a work of great love and care and takes place all over London during many months prior to the carnival, although it must be said that the actual event does not always live up to the vision of the people who create it.

No description of Notting Hill would be complete without mention of Portobello Road. With its antique as well as fruit and vegetable market, Portobello Road is now one of the main tourist attractions of London and what most visitors to London associate with Notting Hill. The street, which originally started at Notting Hill Gate as a country lane called Portobello Lane, derives its name from a port in Colombia (then belonging to Spain) in the Caribbean, Puerto Bello. This city was captured by Admiral Vernon in 1739 and such was the jubilation in England that a medal of Admiral Vernon was struck. Today the Admiral is commemorated on Portobello Road by a cul-de-sac, Vernon's Yard, and a building, the Admiral Vernon, which was formerly a pub and now houses several dozen antique stalls.

The street market started in the late 1860s, as a fruit and vegetable market, and in the 1870s Saturday nights in winter were carnival time in the market. The antique and bric-à-brac dealers set up their stalls much later, in the early twentieth century, with the whole market becoming increasingly popular after the Second World War. I have heard it said that dealers with West End shops make more money on Saturdays in Portobello Road than during the rest of the week in their smarter establishments. On Saturday mornings from about 8 a.m. there can be seen a trickle of early risers moving from Notting Hill Gate down the couple of hundred yards of Pembridge Road and turning left on to the top end of Portobello Road. By 10.30 a.m. this trickle has become a flood of people hoping to pick up a bargain and attracted by the general holiday atmosphere.

After its period of decline, for a long time Notting Hill was appreciated by only a relatively small number of people. The perception of change really began in the late 1960s. In his book *Notting Hill in Bygone Days*, written in 1969, Ashley Barker wrote, 'the powers of recovery of a district so interestingly conceived as the better part of Notting Hill should not be too easily discounted.' By the mid-1970s the area was well on the way to recovery, although still relatively unfashionable. I was told when we moved here that it was referred to by some estate agents as the 'English ghetto' and as late as 1993 one of the most successful antique dealers, who had his shop in Westbourne Grove, would refer to the street as Westbourne Grave.

Today, in many ways the area is in danger of becoming a victim of its own success, with local shops being squeezed out by boutiques – even the post office in Westbourne Grove has suffered this fate – and the native inhabitants of the 'English ghetto' being gradually supplanted, at least to a certain extent, by foreign millionaires and modern-day celebrities.

However, all is not gloom in Notting Hill: the influx of new money and rising property prices have meant that many of the houses of the Ladbroke estate have been brought back to fine health, as have all the communal gardens, many of which have been meticulously restored, with the help of old planting plans and drawings, to their original Victorian designs. It should not be forgotten that in the early years, with the half-abandoned terraces struggling towards completion, the gardens were only just planted out; and by the time the trees had reached maturity the buildings were becoming neglected. Today, with the trees and gardens in their prime and the buildings properly cared for, the original vision of Thomas Allason is probably nearer realization than at any previous time in Notting Hill's chequered history.

Behind the Coronet Cinema on the north side of Notting Hill Gate. These houses would have been built as workmen's or artisans' cottages.

The south side of Ladbroke Square, built before the grander ones on the north side of the Square

The sense of infinity implied
by the vista of these streets
holds the key to Notting Hill's
architectural appeal.

An early walker in one of Notting
Hill's largest private squares

Late afternoon in the same square

There is nothing reticent
about these railings in
Ladbroke Gardens: they
exude self-confidence.

When this architecturally undistinguished late-nineteenth-century church was sold to a property company in 2000 there were fears that the proposed block of flats that was to replace it would be even less impressive. However, thanks to local pressure, the company was obliged to modify its design and even added the twin spires that had been intended for the original building but never realized. The spires provide a welcome eye-catcher on the corner of Westbourne Grove and Ledbury Road – a rare example of development improving an existing building.

Notting Hill Gate, the 'gate' part of the name referring to the toll-gate that once stood at this point, where the Uxbridge Road – now Holland Park Avenue – started in the early nineteenth century. The harsh buildings seen in this photograph are the fruits of 1960s planning, something most of Notting Hill was mercifully spared.

Street behind the Gate and
Coronet cinemas at Notting
Hill Gate

A mews that has retained
its cobblestones

The Earl of Lonsdale pub, named after the colourful peer of that name, known as 'the boxing earl'. He was the founder of the Lonsdale Belt, a trophy highly regarded by boxing enthusiasts.

Notting Hill Gate boasts two cinemas within a hundred yards of each other: this one, the Coronet, and the Gate. The Gate's exterior is of no architectural interest; however, in its choice of programmes it is London's most adventurous cinema. Though originally built as a theatre in 1898, before Edward VII became king, the Coronet is a fine example of what is known as Edwardian architecture.

The Coronet Cinema. Used variously as a theatre and a variety hall, the Coronet became a cinema in 1923 and has remained one ever since. It was the last cinema in London to allow smoking in its auditorium.

OPPOSITE
**Swingtime in a Notting
Hill square**

BELOW
**Another private square,
with pavilion**

ABOVE
'. . . schoolboys from their books'

St Peter's Church in
Kensington Park Road,
'Borromini in Nottting Hill'

THE ROYAL BOROUGH OF KENSINGTON & CHELSEA

ST. PETER'S CHURCH

ONE OF THE LAST CHURCHES BUILT FOR THE CHURCH
OF ENGLAND IN THE VICTORIAN CLASSICAL STYLE.
THE ARCHITECT WAS THOMAS ALLOM WHO
DESIGNED STANLEY GARDENS OPPOSITE AND IT
WAS CONSECRATED ON 7TH JANUARY 1857. THE
MAGNIFICENT INTERIOR WAS FURTHER EMBELLISHED
IN 1879 BY CHARLES BARRY JNR., SON OF THE
ARCHITECT OF THE HOUSES OF PARLIAMENT.

Looking down Stanley Gardens to St Peter's Church. Its honey colour makes a pleasing contrast with the white stucco of the surrounding streets.

The spire of St John's Church
seen from Lansdowne Rise

An early April morning before
the dew has dried

Helen Brunner, famed Suzuki violin teacher, with one of her older pupils – most start before they are three years old.

St John's Church. From this spot in the early nineteenth century could be seen both St Paul's to the east and Windsor Castle, some twenty miles to the west.

This rose was photographed not in an English garden but hanging over a wall off the Portobello Road.

BELOW
One of London's few (thirteen) remaining 'cabmen's shelters'. These were built in 1874 thanks to the generosity of a group of people headed by the Earl of Shaftesbury. The aim was 'to provide cabbies with good and wholesome refreshments at moderate prices'. Because the shelters stood on a public highway the rules stipulated that they were not to be larger than a horse and cart. Gambling, drinking and swearing were strictly forbidden.

LEFT

Looking up Holland Park Avenue toward Notting Hill Gate. The great plane trees that line this road have mercifully been spared pollarding and provide a graceful canopy.

OPPOSITE

Ladbroke Grove, looking towards Holland Park Avenue

In most cities of the world
nature is kept firmly in check.
In Notting Hill nature spills
out on to the street.

Architectural boldness
characteristic of houses built
by Thomas Allom

Looking from Kensington Park
Gardens down Stanley Crescent

What a good stage designer Thomas Allom would have been! There is a real theatricality in the layout and juxtaposition of the houses.

Note the graceful window pelmets; also the sculptural boldness of the architecture.

OPPOSITE
Terrace in St Stephen's Gardens

RIGHT
**The south side of Ladbroke
Square, whose vista creates a
sense of distance beyond**

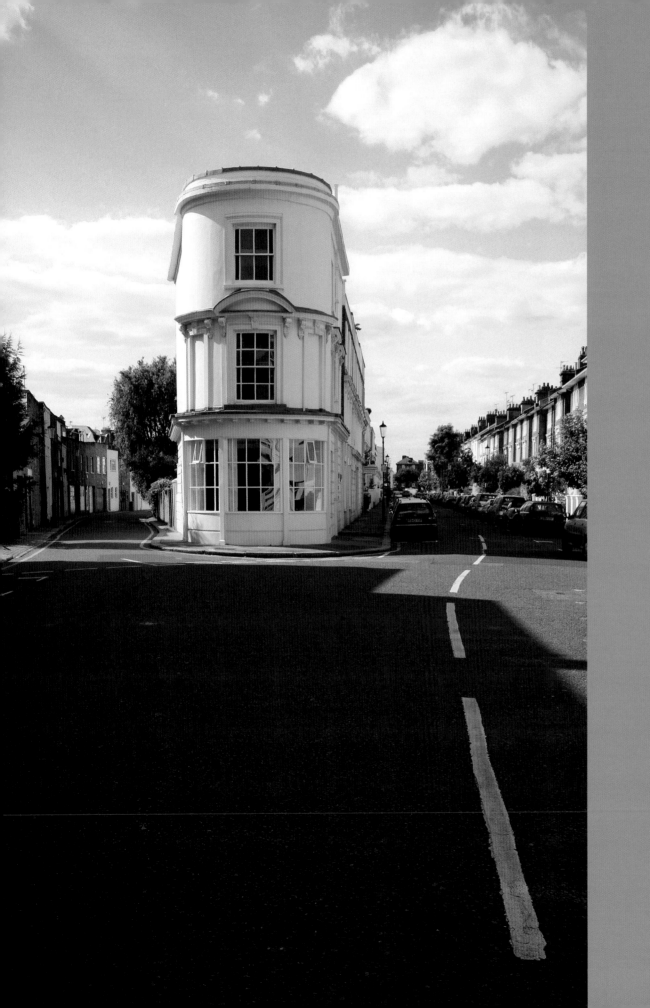

Slim elegance

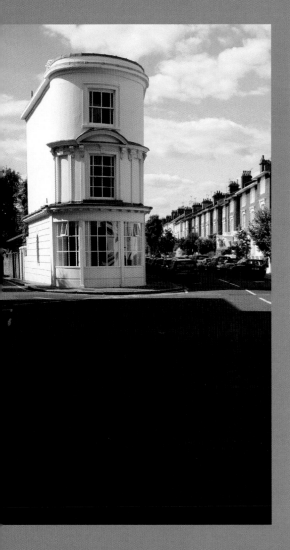

BELOW
First tennis lesson

Two examples of the distinctive corner buildings that are a feature of Notting Hill.

LEFT
At the junction of Westbourne Grove and Pembridge Villas.

OPPOSITE
Where Pembridge Road and Kensington Park Road meet Notting Hill Gate. In 1840 the entrance to the Hippodrome racecourse stood at this spot.

This juction near Clarendon Cross is another example of the surprises to be found in the layout of the streets of the area.

OPPOSITE
Ladbroke Road. Note the convex curve and the fine wrought iron window box holders.

LEFT
How the wisteria not only enhances this window, but lends it a touch of mystery.

The playwright Simon Gray in
Daunt's bookshop – a dangerous
place where people go in to buy
one book and come out with five
they hadn't realized they wanted!

OPPOSITE
Path along Campden Hill Square.
Note the generous iron supports
for the railings.

OPPOSITE
What grace in this Regency
balcony on Holland Park Avenue!

RIGHT
This house on Holland Park
Avenue, built in the early 1840s,
is a good example of the
architecture of the early part of
Notting Hill's development.

OPPOSITE

Gianfranco Antichi, the owner of one of the few surviving antique shops in Ledbury Road, came to England from his native Florence in 1953 to learn English. Horrified by the bad food and the fog, both of which prevailed at that time, he went home to Italy. However to his surprise he felt a certain nostalgia for London, returned, and has lived here ever since.

On Holland Park Avenue, these houses have something of *La Belle au Bois Dormant* about them.

BELOW
**Notting Hill interior. With
exquisite taste, the owner
manages to give a sense of
grandeur to this tiny flat.**

OPPOSITE
Colin Lacy and his son, David, in their
shop, the Lacy Gallery, which specializes
in antique frames. Colin Lacy started
selling frames in 1960 from a barrow in the
Portobello Road. He opened a small shop
in Ledbury Road in 1968 and now he and
his son have an entire house round the
corner in Westbourne Grove, a shop that
attracts customers from around the globe.

Early morning light lends elegance to the reassuring solidity of Ladbroke Gardens' ironwork.

White and cream stucco
calms the ebullience of
these buildings.

The one surviving pottery
kiln, preserved as a
monument on the edge of
what was once the notorious
Notting Dale, one of
London's worst slums

More *rus in urbe*

OPPOSITE

Mr David Lidgate outside his shop,
C Lidgate, on Holland Park Avenue.
The business was founded by his
great-grandfather Charles Lidgate in
1850 and holds a well justified
reputation as the best butcher in
west London. David Lidgate's two
sons both work in the business.

BELOW

The Michanicou brothers, Andy and
Chris, started their shop round the
corner from Holland Park Avenue in
1982. In 1985 the borough council tried
to stop them having their produce
displayed on the pavement, an order
that would have been fatal for their
business. Luckily, such was the local
outcry that the council was obliged to
back down. This shop sells the finest
fruit and vegetables in London.

The top of Pembridge Road
where it meets Notting Hill
Gate has preserved much of
its raffish quality.

Looking up Portobello Road before the crowds arrive. The spire of St Peter's Church can be glimpsed above the houses.

LEFT AND RIGHT
**Clothing stalls in Portobello
Market on Saturday morning**

OVERLEAF
Market produce on a Saturday

Breakfast on
Westbourne Grove

RIGHT AND OPPOSITE
Portobello Market on Saturday

OVERLEAF
**March past in the Market on
Saturday morning**

Preparing for the school play

LEFT
Arthur presides over one of
the workshops where the
Carnival costumes are made.

OPPOSITE
Carnival headdress.

Carnival costumes

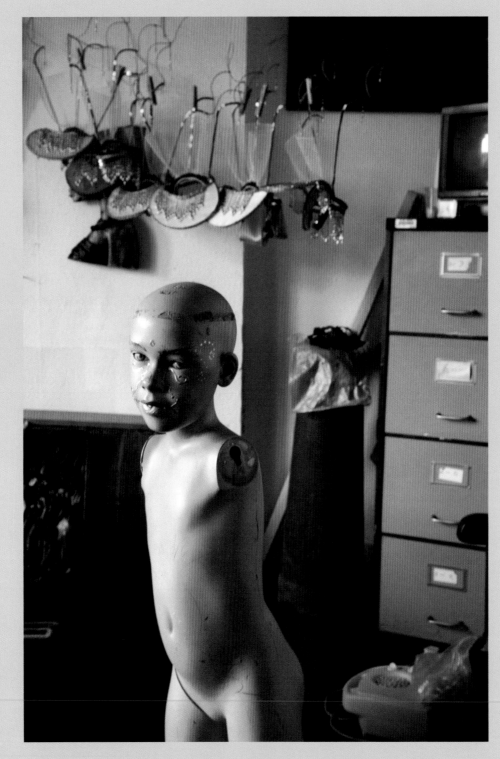

LEFT
Larry Ford, who designs
and makes costumes,
working lovingly on one
of the headpieces

LEFT
**A girl from one of
London's art schools
making carnival costumes**

OPPOSITE
Carnival costume

Carnival morning

Index

Entries in *italics* refer to illustrations.

Acknowledgements

While I am indebted to many people for their help, I would especially like to thank Mr Ashley Barker, perhaps the greatest expert on the history of Notting Hill, who has been particularly generous in the way in which he has shared his knowledge.

I would also like to thank Mr David Barclay, not only for introducing me to Ashley Barker, but also for helping with the later history of Notting Hill.

Becky Clarke, who has done the layout of this book, has shown great tolerance towards my vacillations, as has Jo Christian, my editor, who has nudged the book to completion with great patience and encouragement.